Editor in Chief
Karen J. Goldfluss, M.S. Ed.

Creative Director
Sarah M. Fournier

Cover Artist
Sarah Kim

Imaging
Amanda R. Harter

Illustrator
Kelly McMahon

Publisher
Mary D. Smith, M.S. Ed.

Sight Words

1

TCR 8049

1. Strengthens each student's ability to identify, understand, and use common sight words

2. Develops and reinforces correct spelling and word formation

3. Includes flash cards of words for practice opportunities

Teacher Created Resources

Author
Erica N. Russikoff, M.A.

Teacher Created Resources
12621 Western Avenue
Garden Grove, CA 92841
www.teachercreated.com

ISBN: 978-1-4206-8049-2

©2018 Teacher Created Resources
Reprinted, 2019
Made in U.S.A.

Teacher Created Resources

Table of Contents

Introduction

Sight words are the most frequently used words in reading and writing. They are called "sight words" because they must be recognized instantly, on sight, for reading fluency. Many sight words do not follow standard phonics rules or spelling patterns, which makes them difficult for early readers to recognize, sound out, and comprehend. In this book, 100 sight words are provided for practice. Words 1–50 are intended for kindergarten students, while words 51–100 are intended for first-grade students. The words are organized by Dr. Fry's order of frequency, with the word *the* being the most frequently used word in the English language. The words can be taught sequentially, but, depending on what an individual student needs, a teacher can choose to skip some words or teach some words before others.

Each word is introduced and taught individually. A series of exercises develops, reinforces, and strengthens students' ability to do the following:

- follow directions

- recognize the words on sight

- read the words in context

- write the words with correct spelling

- identify the letters in the words

- write the words with proper letter formation

- use the written-out words in sentences

Additional activities, starting on page 105, encourage students to choose the correct sight word from two choices. All of the answer choices (sight words) can be found in this book. These activities provide extra practice for students who are familiar with sight words and want to continue their learning.

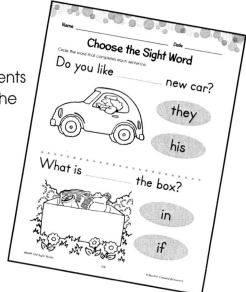

The flash cards at the back of this book can be used for reinforcement and testing. Consider punching holes through them so that the cards can be held together by a string or binder ring.

The activities in this book have been aligned to the Common Core State Standards for Language Arts. These standards can be found on the last page of this book.

How to Use This Book

The following exercises are included in this book:

Tracing and Writing the Word

This activity allows students to recognize a new sight word. When students trace a word, they become familiar with the letters and sequence that make up the new word. This activity also invites students to practice their letter formation.

Circling the Word's Letters from the Alphabet

This activity reinforces alphabet sequence while providing an opportunity for visual matching. Additionally, it helps students realize the manageability of language, in that every word will be formed from these same 26 letters—regardless of the number of letters a word contains and what the letters are.

Finding the Box the Word Fits Into

This activity allows students to focus on the shape of the new sight word. It invites students to think about how the letters fit against each other—whether letters go above or below the line and whether those upward or downward letters go at the beginning or end of the word.

Writing the Word in a Sentence

This activity encourages students to practice writing the new sight word in a sentence. The sentence appears twice on the page. The first appearance is in the top, right-hand side of the page. The sentence includes the sight word with a related picture. The sentence appears a second time at the bottom of the page, where students are asked to complete the sentence by writing the sight word in question. *Note:* Sometimes the word is used at the beginning of the sentence. (See page 12 for an example.) In these cases, the capital letter will need to be taught and practiced.

SIGHT WORD

the

Trace the word **the**.

the   the

Write the word **the** on the lines.

He ate **the** apple.

Circle the letters from the alphabet found in the word **the**.

a b c d e f g h i j k l m n o p q r s t u v w x y z

Find the set of boxes that **the** fits into. Write **the** in the correct set of boxes.

Write the word to finish this sentence.

He ate _____ apple.

SIGHT WORD   # of

Trace the word **of**.

of   of   of

Write the word **of** on the lines.

Look at the piece
of cake.

Circle the letters from the alphabet found in the word **of**.

a b c d e f g h i j k l m n o p q r s t u v w x y z

Find the set of boxes that **of** fits into. Write **of** in the correct set of boxes.

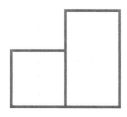      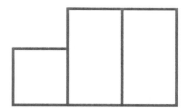

Write the word to finish this sentence.

Look at the piece _____ cake.

SIGHT WORD

and

Trace the word **and**.

and and

Write the word **and** on the lines.

_____ _____

_____ _____

_____ _____

_____ _____

She has a dog
and a cat.

Circle the letters from the alphabet found in the word **and**.

a b c d e f g h i j k l m n o p q r s t u v w x y z

Find the set of boxes that **and** fits into. Write **and** in the correct set of boxes.

Write the word to finish this sentence.

She has a dog _____ a cat.

SIGHT WORD

a

Trace the word **a**.

a a a a

Write the word **a** on the lines.

_____ _____

_____ _____

_____ _____

I use **a** pencil.

Circle the letter from the alphabet found in the word **a**.

a b c d e f g h i j k l m n o p q r s t u v w x y z

Find the box that **a** fits into. Write **a** in the correct box.

Write the word to finish this sentence.

I use _____ pencil.

SIGHT WORD

to

Trace the word **to**.

to   to   to

Write the word **to** on the lines.

SCHOOL

They go **to** school.

Circle the letters from the alphabet found in the word **to**.

a b c d e f g h i j k l m n o p q r s t u v w x y z

Find the set of boxes that **to** fits into. Write **to** in the correct set of boxes.

Write the word to finish this sentence.

They go _____ school.

SIGHT WORD

in

Trace the word **in**.

in   in   in

Write the word **in** on the lines.

_____   _____

_____   _____

_____   _____

Fish live **in** the ocean.

Circle the letters from the alphabet found in the word **in**.

a b c d e f g h i j k l m n o p q r s t u v w x y z

Find the set of boxes that **in** fits into. Write **in** in the correct set of boxes.

Write the word to finish this sentence.

Fish live _____ the ocean.

SIGHT WORD

is

Trace the word **is**.

is   is   is

Write the word **is** on the lines.

That car **is** fast!

Circle the letters from the alphabet found in the word **is**.

a b c d e f g h i j k l m n o p q r s t u v w x y z

Find the set of boxes that **is** fits into. Write **is** in the correct set of boxes.

Write the word to finish this sentence.

That car _____ fast!

SIGHT WORD

you

Trace the word **you**.

you   you

Write the word **you** on the lines.

You have two feet.

Circle the letters from the alphabet found in the word **you**.

a b c d e f g h i j k l m n o p q r s t u v w x y z

Find the set of boxes that **you** fits into. Write **you** in the correct set of boxes.

Write the word to finish this sentence.

_____ have two feet.

SIGHT WORD

that

Trace the word **that**.

that that

Write the word **that** on the lines.

_____   _____

_____   _____

_____   _____

Is that a flag?

Circle the letters from the alphabet found in the word **that**.

a b c d e f g h i j k l m n o p q r s t u v w x y z

Find the set of boxes that **that** fits into. Write **that** in the correct set of boxes.

Write the word to finish this sentence.

Is _____ a flag?

SIGHT WORD

it

Trace the word **it**.

_____

it   it   it

Write the word **it** on the lines.

_____ _____

_____ _____

_____ _____

_____ _____

What time is **it**?

Circle the letters from the alphabet found in the word **it**.

a b c d e f g h i j k l m n o p q r s t u v w x y z

Find the set of boxes that **it** fits into. Write **it** in the correct set of boxes.

Write the word to finish this sentence.

What time is _____?

SIGHT WORD

he

Trace the word **he**.

he he he

Write the word **he** on the lines.

_____   _____

_____   _____

_____   _____

He took a bath.

Circle the letters from the alphabet found in the word **he**.

a b c d e f g h i j k l m n o p q r s t u v w x y z

Find the set of boxes that **he** fits into. Write **he** in the correct set of boxes.

Write the word to finish this sentence.

_____ took a bath.

SIGHT WORD

was

Trace the word **was**.

was was

Write the word **was** on the lines.

_____ _____

_____ _____

_____ _____

I **was** doing work.

Circle the letters from the alphabet found in the word **was**.

a b c d e f g h i j k l m n o p q r s t u v w x y z

Find the set of boxes that **was** fits into. Write **was** in the correct set of boxes.

Write the word to finish this sentence.

I _____ doing work.

SIGHT WORD

for

Trace the word **for**.

for   for

Write the word **for** on the lines.

_____   _____

_____   _____

_____   _____

That present
is **for** me.

Circle the letters from the alphabet found in the word **for**.

a b c d e f g h i j k l m n o p q r s t u v w x y z

Find the set of boxes that **for** fits into. Write **for** in the correct set of boxes.

Write the word to finish this sentence.

That present is _____ me.

SIGHT WORD

on

Trace the word **on**.

on on on

Write the word **on** on the lines.

_____ _____

_____ _____

_____ _____

_____ _____

Put the flowers **on** the table.

Circle the letters from the alphabet found in the word **on**.

a b c d e f g h i j k l m n o p q r s t u v w x y z

Find the set of boxes that **on** fits into. Write **on** in the correct set of boxes.

Write the word to finish this sentence.

Put the flowers _____ the table.

SIGHT WORD

are

Trace the word **are**.

are   are

Write the word **are** on the lines.

_____   _____

_____   _____

_____   _____

There **are** two birds.

Circle the letters from the alphabet found in the word **are**.

a b c d e f g h i j k l m n o p q r s t u v w x y z

Find the set of boxes that **are** fits into. Write **are** in the correct set of boxes.

Write the word to finish this sentence.

There _____ two birds.

SIGHT WORD

as

Trace the word **as**.

as as as

Write the word **as** on the lines.

_____   _____

_____   _____

_____   _____

_____   _____

The kids played
as it rained.

Circle the letters from the alphabet found in the word **as**.

a b c d e f g h i j k l m n o p q r s t u v w x y z

Find the set of boxes that **as** fits into. Write **as** in the correct set of boxes.

Write the word to finish this sentence.

The kids played _____ it rained.

SIGHT WORD

with

Trace the word **with**.

with with

Write the word **with** on the lines.

I like toast **with** jam.

Circle the letters from the alphabet found in the word **with**.

a b c d e f g h i j k l m n o p q r s t u v w x y z

Find the set of boxes that **with** fits into. Write **with** in the correct set of boxes.

Write the word to finish this sentence.

I like toast _____ jam.

SIGHT WORD

his

Trace the word **his**.

his his his

Write the word **his** on the lines.

His room is clean.

Circle the letters from the alphabet found in the word **his**.

a b c d e f g h i j k l m n o p q r s t u v w x y z

Find the set of boxes that **his** fits into. Write **his** in the correct set of boxes.

Write the word to finish this sentence.

_____ room is clean.

Name _____   Date _____

they

Trace the word **they**.

they they

Write the word **they** on the lines.

_____ _____

_____ _____

_____ _____

_____ _____

They crossed the street.

Circle the letters from the alphabet found in the word **they**.

a b c d e f g h i j k l m n o p q r s t u v w x y z

Find the set of boxes that **they** fits into. Write **they** in the correct set of boxes.

Write the word to finish this sentence.

_____

_____ crossed the street.

SIGHT WORD

I

Trace the word I.

I I I I

Write the word I on the lines.

_____ _____

_____ _____

_____ _____

_____ _____

_____ _____

I drew a picture.

Circle the letter from the alphabet found in the word I.

a b c d e f g h i j k l m n o p q r s t u v w x y z

Find the box that I fits into. Write I in the correct box.

Write the word to finish this sentence.

_____ drew a picture.

SIGHT WORD

at

Trace the word **at**.

at   at   at

Write the word **at** on the lines.

She smiled **at** the dog.

Circle the letters from the alphabet found in the word **at**.

a b c d e f g h i j k l m n o p q r s t u v w x y z

Find the set of boxes that **at** fits into. Write **at** in the correct set of boxes.

Write the word to finish this sentence.

She smiled _____ the dog.

SIGHT WORD

be

Trace the word **be**.

be be be

Write the word **be** on the lines.

_____ _____

_____ _____

_____ _____

The turkey will
be ready soon.

Circle the letters from the alphabet found in the word **be**.

a b c d e f g h i j k l m n o p q r s t u v w x y z

Find the set of boxes that **be** fits into. Write **be** in the correct set of boxes.

Write the word to finish this sentence.

The turkey will _____ ready soon.

SIGHT WORD

this

Trace the word **this**.

this   this

Write the word **this** on the lines.

This is my favorite toy.

Circle the letters from the alphabet found in the word **this**.

a b c d e f g h i j k l m n o p q r s t u v w x y z

Find the set of boxes that **this** fits into. Write **this** in the correct set of boxes.

Write the word to finish this sentence.

_____ is my favorite toy.

SIGHT WORD

have

Trace the word **have**.

have have

Write the word **have** on the lines.

I **have** a cold.

Circle the letters from the alphabet found in the word **have**.

a b c d e f g h i j k l m n o p q r s t u v w x y z

Find the set of boxes that **have** fits into. Write **have** in the correct set of boxes.

Write the word to finish this sentence.

I _____ a cold.

SIGHT WORD

from

Trace the word **from**.

from from

Write the word **from** on the lines.

The letter is **from** my uncle.

Circle the letters from the alphabet found in the word **from**.

a b c d e f g h i j k l m n o p q r s t u v w x y z

Find the set of boxes that **from** fits into. Write **from** in the correct set of boxes.

Write the word to finish this sentence.

The letter is _____ my uncle.

SIGHT WORD

or

Trace the word **or**.

_____

or   or   or

Write the word **or** on the lines.

_____ _____

_____ _____

_____ _____

Do you like
dogs **or** cats?

Circle the letters from the alphabet found in the word **or**.

a b c d e f g h i j k l m n o p q r s t u v w x y z

Find the set of boxes that **or** fits into. Write **or** in the correct set of boxes.

Write the word to finish this sentence.

Do you like dogs _____ cats?

SIGHT WORD

one

Trace the word **one**.

one   one

Write the word **one** on the lines.

We saw **one** boat.

Circle the letters from the alphabet found in the word **one**.

a b c d e f g h i j k l m n o p q r s t u v w x y z

Find the set of boxes that **one** fits into. Write **one** in the correct set of boxes.

Write the word to finish this sentence.

We saw _____ boat.

SIGHT WORD # had

Trace the word **had**.

had had

Write the word **had** on the lines.

_____   _____

I **had** a birthday party.

Circle the letters from the alphabet found in the word **had**.

a b c d e f g h i j k l m n o p q r s t u v w x y z

Find the set of boxes that **had** fits into. Write **had** in the correct set of boxes.

Write the word to finish this sentence.

I _____ a birthday party.

SIGHT WORD

by

Trace the word **by**.

by by by

Write the word **by** on the lines.

She sits **by** Matt.

Circle the letters from the alphabet found in the word **by**.

a b c d e f g h i j k l m n o p q r s t u v w x y z

Find the set of boxes that **by** fits into. Write **by** in the correct set of boxes.

Write the word to finish this sentence.

She sits _____ Matt.

Name _____ Date _____

words

Trace the word **words**.

words words

Write the word **words** on the lines.

_____ _____

_____ _____

_____ _____

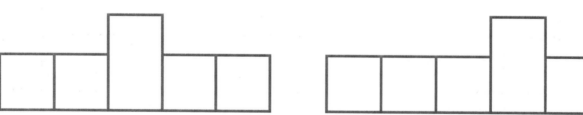

There are many **words** in books.

Circle the letters from the alphabet found in the word **words**.

a b c d e f g h i j k l m n o p q r s t u v w x y z

Find the set of boxes that **words** fits into. Write **words** in the correct set of boxes.

Write the word to finish this sentence. _____

There are many _____ in books.

Name _____   Date _____

but

Trace the word **but**.

but   but

Write the word **but** on the lines.

_____   _____

_____   _____

_____   _____

They were happy but tired.

Circle the letters from the alphabet found in the word **but**.

a b c d e f g h i j k l m n o p q r s t u v w x y z

Find the set of boxes that **but** fits into. Write **but** in the correct set of boxes.

Write the word to finish this sentence.

They were happy _____ tired.

Name _____   Date _____

not

Trace the word **not**.

not   not

Write the word **not** on the lines.

I do **not** like washing dishes.

Circle the letters from the alphabet found in the word **not**.

a b c d e f g h i j k l m n o p q r s t u v w x y z

Find the set of boxes that **not** fits into. Write **not** in the correct set of boxes.

Write the word to finish this sentence.

I do _____ like washing dishes.

SIGHT WORD

what

Trace the word **what**.

what what

Write the word **what** on the lines.

What did you bring for lunch?

Circle the letters from the alphabet found in the word **what**.

a b c d e f g h i j k l m n o p q r s t u v w x y z

Find the set of boxes that **what** fits into. Write **what** in the correct set of boxes.

Write the word to finish this sentence.

_____ did you bring for lunch?

SIGHT WORD

all

Trace the word **all**.

all all all

Write the word **all** on the lines.

_____ _____

_____ _____

They should
all listen.

Circle the letters from the alphabet found in the word **all**.

a b c d e f g h i j k l m n o p q r s t u v w x y z

Find the set of boxes that **all** fits into. Write **all** in the correct set of boxes.

Write the word to finish this sentence.

They should _____ listen.

SIGHT WORD

were

Trace the word **were**.

were were

Write the word **were** on the lines.

They **were** reading.

Circle the letters from the alphabet found in the word **were**.

a b c d e f g h i j k l m n o p q r s t u v w x y z

Find the set of boxes that **were** fits into. Write **were** in the correct set of boxes.

Write the word to finish this sentence.

They _____ reading.

Name _____   Date _____

SIGHT WORD

we

Trace the word **we**.

_____

we we we

_____

Write the word **we** on the lines.

_____   _____

_____   _____

_____   _____

We went to sleep.

Circle the letters from the alphabet found in the word **we**.

a b c d e f g h i j k l m n o p q r s t u v w x y z

Find the set of boxes that **we** fits into. Write **we** in the correct set of boxes.

Write the word to finish this sentence.

_____

_____ went to sleep.

SIGHT WORD

when

Trace the word **when**.

when when

Write the word **when** on the lines.

_____ _____

_____ _____

_____ _____

When do you play baseball?

Circle the letters from the alphabet found in the word **when**.

a b c d e f g h i j k l m n o p q r s t u v w x y z

Find the set of boxes that **when** fits into. Write **when** in the correct set of boxes.

Write the word to finish this sentence.

_____

_____ do you play baseball?

SIGHT WORD

your

Trace the word **your**.

your your

Write the word **your** on the lines.

_____ _____

....

_____ _____

....

What is **your** name?

Circle the letters from the alphabet found in the word **your**.

a b c d e f g h i j k l m n o p q r s t u v w x y z

Find the set of boxes that **your** fits into. Write **your** in the correct set of boxes.

Write the word to finish this sentence.

_____

What is _____ name?

SIGHT WORD

can

Trace the word **can**.

can can

Write the word **can** on the lines.

We **can** dance!

Circle the letters from the alphabet found in the word **can**.

a b c d e f g h i j k l m n o p q r s t u v w x y z

Find the set of boxes that **can** fits into. Write **can** in the correct set of boxes.

Write the word to finish this sentence.

We _____ dance!

SIGHT WORD

said

Trace the word **said**.

said said

Write the word **said** on the lines.

_____ _____

_____ _____

_____ _____

He **said** it was time to eat.

Circle the letters from the alphabet found in the word **said**.

a b c d e f g h i j k l m n o p q r s t u v w x y z

Find the set of boxes that **said** fits into. Write **said** in the correct set of boxes.

Write the word to finish this sentence.

He _____ it was time to eat.

SIGHT WORD

there

Trace the word **there**.

there there

Write the word **there** on the lines.

_____   _____

_____   _____

_____   _____

There is a worm on the hook.

Circle the letters from the alphabet found in the word **there**.

a b c d e f g h i j k l m n o p q r s t u v w x y z

Find the set of boxes that **there** fits into. Write **there** in the correct set of boxes.

Write the word to finish this sentence.

_____ is a worm on the hook.

SIGHT WORD

use

Trace the word **use**.

use use

Write the word **use** on the lines.

Use soap when you wash your hands.

Circle the letters from the alphabet found in the word **use**.

a b c d e f g h i j k l m n o p q r s t u v w x y z

Find the set of boxes that **use** fits into. Write **use** in the correct set of boxes.

Write the word to finish this sentence.

_____ soap when you wash your hands.

SIGHT WORD

an

Trace the word **an**.

an an an

Write the word **an** on the lines.

An orange is round.

Circle the letters from the alphabet found in the word **an**.

a b c d e f g h i j k l m n o p q r s t u v w x y z

Find the set of boxes that **an** fits into. Write **an** in the correct set of boxes.

Write the word to finish this sentence.

_____ orange is round.

SIGHT WORD

each

Trace the word **each**.

each each

Write the word **each** on the lines.

_____   _____

_____   _____

_____   _____

Look at each letter.

Circle the letters from the alphabet found in the word **each**.

a b c d e f g h i j k l m n o p q r s t u v w x y z

Find the set of boxes that **each** fits into. Write **each** in the correct set of boxes.

Write the word to finish this sentence.

Look at _____ letter.

Name _____   Date _____

SIGHT WORD   # which

Trace the word **which**.

which which

Write the word **which** on the lines.

_____ _____

_____ _____

_____ _____

Which one is a sheep?

Circle the letters from the alphabet found in the word **which**.

a b c d e f g h i j k l m n o p q r s t u v w x y z

Find the set of boxes that **which** fits into. Write **which** in the correct set of boxes.

Write the word to finish this sentence.

_____

_____   one is a sheep?

SIGHT WORD

she

Trace the word **she**.

she   she

Write the word **she** on the lines.

She brushed her teeth.

Circle the letters from the alphabet found in the word **she**.

a b c d e f g h i j k l m n o p q r s t u v w x y z

Find the set of boxes that **she** fits into. Write **she** in the correct set of boxes.

Write the word to finish this sentence.

_____ brushed her teeth.

SIGHT WORD   # do

Trace the word **do**.

do do do

Write the word **do** on the lines.

Do you like the rain?

Circle the letters from the alphabet found in the word **do**.

a b c d e f g h i j k l m n o p q r s t u v w x y z

Find the set of boxes that **do** fits into. Write **do** in the correct set of boxes.

Write the word to finish this sentence.

_____ you like the rain?

SIGHT WORD

how

Trace the word **how**.

how how

Write the word **how** on the lines.

_____   _____

_____   _____

_____   _____

How many caps are there?

Circle the letters from the alphabet found in the word **how**.

a b c d e f g h i j k l m n o p q r s t u v w x y z

Find the set of boxes that **how** fits into. Write **how** in the correct set of boxes.

Write the word to finish this sentence.

_____

_____ many caps are there?

SIGHT WORD

their

Trace the word **their**.

their their

Write the word **their** on the lines.

Their bus is late.

Circle the letters from the alphabet found in the word **their**.

a b c d e f g h i j k l m n o p q r s t u v w x y z

Find the set of boxes that **their** fits into. Write **their** in the correct set of boxes.

Write the word to finish this sentence.

bus is late.

SIGH T WORD

if

Trace the word **if**.

if if if if

Write the word **if** on the lines.

Mark

I will bring my lunch **if** I go.

Circle the letters from the alphabet found in the word **if**.

a b c d e f g h i j k l m n o p q r s t u v w x y z

Find the set of boxes that **if** fits into. Write **if** in the correct set of boxes.

Write the word to finish this sentence.

I will bring my lunch _____ I go.

SIGHT WORD

will

Trace the word **will**.

will will

Write the word **will** on the lines.

Who **will** win the race?

Circle the letters from the alphabet found in the word **will**.

a b c d e f g h i j k l m n o p q r s t u v w x y z

Find the set of boxes that **will** fits into. Write **will** in the correct set of boxes.

Write the word to finish this sentence.

Who _____ win the race?

SIGHT WORD

up

Trace the word **up**.

up up up

Write the word **up** on the lines.

The mouse ran
up the clock.

Circle the letters from the alphabet found in the word **up**.

a b c d e f g h i j k l m n o p q r s t u v w x y z

Find the set of boxes that **up** fits into. Write **up** in the correct set of boxes.

Write the word to finish this sentence.

The mouse ran _____ the clock.

SIGHT WORD

other

Trace the word **other**.

other other

Write the word **other** on the lines.

They love each **other**.

Circle the letters from the alphabet found in the word **other**.

a b c d e f g h i j k l m n o p q r s t u v w x y z

Find the set of boxes that **other** fits into. Write **other** in the correct set of boxes.

Write the word to finish this sentence.

They love each _____ .

SIGHT WORD # about

Trace the word **about**.

about about

Write the word **about** on the lines.

What do you
know **about** cows?

Circle the letters from the alphabet found in the word **about**.

a b c d e f g h i j k l m n o p q r s t u v w x y z

Find the set of boxes that **about** fits into. Write **about** in the correct set of boxes.

Write the word to finish this sentence.

What do you know _____ cows?

SIGHT WORD

out

Trace the word **out**.

out   out

Write the word **out** on the lines.

Take the broom **out** and sweep.

Circle the letters from the alphabet found in the word **out**.

a b c d e f g h i j k l m n o p q r s t u v w x y z

Find the set of boxes that **out** fits into. Write **out** in the correct set of boxes.

Write the word to finish this sentence.

Take the broom _____ and sweep.

Name _____ Date _____

SIGHT WORD # many

Trace the word **many**.

many many

Write the word **many** on the lines.

_____   _____

_____   _____

_____   _____

He blew **many** bubbles.

Circle the letters from the alphabet found in the word **many**.

a b c d e f g h i j k l m n o p q r s t u v w x y z

Find the set of boxes that **many** fits into. Write **many** in the correct set of boxes.

Write the word to finish this sentence.

He blew _____ bubbles.

SIGHT WORD

then

Trace the word **then**.

_____

then then

Write the word **then** on the lines.

_____   _____

_____   _____

_____   _____

_____   _____

He moved the chair **then** sat down.

Circle the letters from the alphabet found in the word **then**.

a b c d e f g h i j k l m n o p q r s t u v w x y z

Find the set of boxes that **then** fits into. Write **then** in the correct set of boxes.

Write the word to finish this sentence.   _____

He moved the chair _____ sat down.

Name _____ Date _____

them

Trace the word **them**.

them them

Write the word **them** on the lines.

_____ _____

_____ _____

_____ _____

The bus is taking **them** to school.

Circle the letters from the alphabet found in the word **them**.

a b c d e f g h i j k l m n o p q r s t u v w x y z

Find the set of boxes that **them** fits into. Write **them** in the correct set of boxes.

Write the word to finish this sentence.

The bus is taking _____
to school.

SIGHT WORD

these

Trace the word **these**.

these these

Write the word **these** on the lines.

_____ _____

_____ _____

_____ _____

_____ _____

These flowers need water.

Circle the letters from the alphabet found in the word **these**.

a b c d e f g h i j k l m n o p q r s t u v w x y z

Find the set of boxes that **these** fits into. Write **these** in the correct set of boxes.

Write the word to finish this sentence.

_____

flowers need water.

SIGHT WORD **so**

Trace the word **so**.

so so so

Write the word **so** on the lines.

The cave was **so** dark.

Circle the letters from the alphabet found in the word **so**.

a b c d e f g h i j k l m n o p q r s t u v w x y z

Find the set of boxes that **so** fits into. Write **so** in the correct set of boxes.

Write the word to finish this sentence.

The cave was _____ dark.

SIGHT WORD

some

Trace the word **some**.

some some

Write the word **some** on the lines.

Some bugs fly.

Circle the letters from the alphabet found in the word **some**.

a b c d e f g h i j k l m n o p q r s t u v w x y z

Find the set of boxes that **some** fits into. Write **some** in the correct set of boxes.

Write the word to finish this sentence.

_____

_____ bugs fly.

SIGHT WORD

her

Trace the word **her**.

her   her

Write the word **her** on the lines.

_____   _____

_____   _____

_____   _____

Her card is nice.

Circle the letters from the alphabet found in the word **her**.

a b c d e f g h i j k l m n o p q r s t u v w x y z

Find the set of boxes that **her** fits into. Write **her** in the correct set of boxes.

Write the word to finish this sentence.

_____

_____ card is nice.

SIGHT WORD

would

Trace the word **would**.

would would

Write the word **would** on the lines.

_____   _____

_____   _____

_____   _____

Would you like to walk the dogs?

Circle the letters from the alphabet found in the word **would**.

a b c d e f g h i j k l m n o p q r s t u v w x y z

Find the set of boxes that **would** fits into. Write **would** in the correct set of boxes.

Write the word to finish this sentence.

_____

_____ you like to walk the dogs?

SIGHT WORD

make

Trace the word **make**.

make make

Write the word **make** on the lines.

_____   _____

_____   _____

_____   _____

Make a wish!

Circle the letters from the alphabet found in the word **make**.

a b c d e f g h i j k l m n o p q r s t u v w x y z

Find the set of boxes that **make** fits into. Write **make** in the correct set of boxes.

Write the word to finish this sentence.

_____ a wish!

Name _____   Date _____

like

Trace the word **like**.

like   like

Write the word **like** on the lines.

_____   _____

_____   _____

_____   _____

Do you **like** fruit?

Circle the letters from the alphabet found in the word **like**.

a b c d e f g h i j k l m n o p q r s t u v w x y z

Find the set of boxes that **like** fits into. Write **like** in the correct set of boxes.

Write the word to finish this sentence.

_____

Do you _____ fruit?

SIGHT WORD

him

Trace the word **him**.

him him

Write the word **him** on the lines.

_____   _____

_____   _____

_____   _____

_____   _____

Watch **him** throw the balls!

Circle the letters from the alphabet found in the word **him**.

a b c d e f g h i j k l m n o p q r s t u v w x y z

Find the set of boxes that **him** fits into. Write **him** in the correct set of boxes.

Write the word to finish this sentence.

Watch _____ throw the balls!

SIGHT WORD

into

Trace the word **into**.

into into

Write the word **into** on the lines.

Put the bird **into** the cage.

Circle the letters from the alphabet found in the word **into**.

a b c d e f g h i j k l m n o p q r s t u v w x y z

Find the set of boxes that **into** fits into. Write **into** in the correct set of boxes.

Write the word to finish this sentence.

Put the bird _____ the cage.

SIGHT WORD

time

Trace the word **time**.

time time

Write the word **time** on the lines.

_____   _____

_____   _____

_____   _____

Time to run!

Circle the letters from the alphabet found in the word **time**.

a b c d e f g h i j k l m n o p q r s t u v w x y z

Find the set of boxes that **time** fits into. Write **time** in the correct set of boxes.

Write the word to finish this sentence.

_____

_____ to run!

SIGHT WORD

has

Trace the word **has**.

has   has

Write the word **has** on the lines.

_____   _____

_____   _____

_____   _____

The bunny **has** a tail.

Circle the letters from the alphabet found in the word **has**.

a b c d e f g h i j k l m n o p q r s t u v w x y z

Find the set of boxes that **has** fits into. Write **has** in the correct set of boxes.

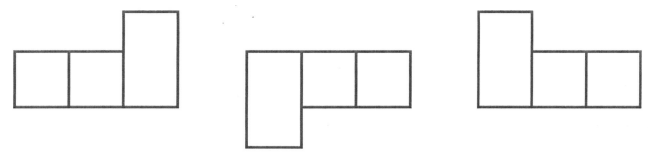

Write the word to finish this sentence.

The bunny _____ a tail.

Name _____   Date _____

look

Trace the word **look**.

look look

Write the word **look** on the lines.

_____   _____

_____   _____

_____   _____

Look at that frog!

Circle the letters from the alphabet found in the word **look**.

a b c d e f g h i j k l m n o p q r s t u v w x y z

Find the set of boxes that **look** fits into. Write **look** in the correct set of boxes.

Write the word to finish this sentence.

_____

_____ at that frog!

SIGHT WORD

two

Trace the word **two**.

two two

Write the word **two** on the lines.

_____ _____

_____ _____

_____ _____

Two more buttons to go!

Circle the letters from the alphabet found in the word **two**.

a b c d e f g h i j k l m n o p q r s t u v w x y z

Find the set of boxes that **two** fits into. Write **two** in the correct set of boxes.

Write the word to finish this sentence.

_____ more buttons to go!

Name _____ Date _____

more

Trace the word **more**.

more more

Write the word **more** on the lines.

_____   _____
_____   _____
_____   _____
_____   _____

Do you
want **more**?

Circle the letters from the alphabet found in the word **more**.

a b c d e f g h i j k l m n o p q r s t u v w x y z

Find the set of boxes that **more** fits into. Write **more** in the correct set of boxes.

Write the word to finish this sentence.

Do you want _____ ?

SIGHT WORD

write

Trace the word **write**.

_____

write write

_____

Write the word **write** on the lines.

_____   _____

_____   _____

_____   _____

What will she **write**?

Circle the letters from the alphabet found in the word **write**.

a b c d e f g h i j k l m n o p q r s t u v w x y z

Find the set of boxes that **write** fits into. Write **write** in the correct set of boxes.

Write the word to finish this sentence.

What will she _____?

SIGHT WORD

go

Trace the word **go**.

go go go

Write the word **go** on the lines.

Should I stop or **go**?

Circle the letters from the alphabet found in the word **go**.

a b c d e f g h i j k l m n o p q r s t u v w x y z

Find the set of boxes that **go** fits into. Write **go** in the correct set of boxes.

Write the word to finish this sentence.

Should I stop or _____?

SIGHT WORD

see

Trace the word **see**.

_____

see see

_____

Write the word **see** on the lines.

_____ _____

_____ _____

_____ _____

What do you **see**?

Circle the letters from the alphabet found in the word **see**.

a b c d e f g h i j k l m n o p q r s t u v w x y z

Find the set of boxes that **see** fits into. Write **see** in the correct set of boxes.

Write the word to finish this sentence.

What do you _____?

SIGHT WORD

number

Trace the word **number**.

number

Write the word **number** on the lines.

What **number** is this?

Circle the letters from the alphabet found in the word **number**.

a b c d e f g h i j k l m n o p q r s t u v w x y z

Find the set of boxes that **number** fits into. Write **number** in the correct set of boxes.

Write the word to finish this sentence.

What _____ is this?

SIGHT WORD

no

Trace the word **no**.

no no no

Write the word **no** on the lines.

This house
has **no** door.

Circle the letters from the alphabet found in the word **no**.

a b c d e f g h i j k l m n o p q r s t u v w x y z

Find the set of boxes that **no** fits into. Write **no** in the correct set of boxes.

Write the word to finish this sentence.

This house has _____ door.

Name _____ Date _____

SIGHT WORD

way

Trace the word **way**.

_____

way way

_____

Write the word **way** on the lines.

_____ _____

_____ _____

_____ _____

Which **way** do I go?

Circle the letters from the alphabet found in the word **way**.

a b c d e f g h i j k l m n o p q r s t u v w x y z

Find the set of boxes that **way** fits into. Write **way** in the correct set of boxes.

Write the word to finish this sentence.

_____

Which _____ do I go?

SIGHT WORD

could

Trace the word **could**.

could could

Write the word **could** on the lines.

Could they be friends?

Circle the letters from the alphabet found in the word **could**.

a b c d e f g h i j k l m n o p q r s t u v w x y z

Find the set of boxes that **could** fits into. Write **could** in the correct set of boxes.

Write the word to finish this sentence.

_____ they be friends?

SIGHT WORD

people

Trace the word **people**.

people

Write the word **people** on the lines.

Help other **people**.

Circle the letters from the alphabet found in the word **people**.

a b c d e f g h i j k l m n o p q r s t u v w x y z

Find the set of boxes that **people** fits into. Write **people** in the correct set of boxes.

Write the word to finish this sentence.

Help other _____.

SIGHT WORD

my

Trace the word **my**.

my   my

Write the word **my** on the lines.

Can you hear
my heart?

thump thump thump

Circle the letters from the alphabet found in the word **my**.

a b c d e f g h i j k l m n o p q r s t u v w x y z

Find the set of boxes that **my** fits into. Write **my** in the correct set of boxes.

Write the word to finish this sentence.

Can you hear _____ heart?

SIGHT WORD

than

Trace the word **than**.

than than

Write the word **than** on the lines.

_____ _____

_____ _____

_____ _____

There are more **than** four ducks.

Circle the letters from the alphabet found in the word **than**.

a b c d e f g h i j k l m n o p q r s t u v w x y z

Find the set of boxes that **than** fits into. Write **than** in the correct set of boxes.

Write the word to finish this sentence.

_____

There are more _____ four ducks.

SIGHT WORD

first

Trace the word **first**.

first first

Write the word **first** on the lines.

_____ _____

_____ _____

_____ _____

The **first** girl has the most hair.

Circle the letters from the alphabet found in the word **first**.

a b c d e f g h i j k l m n o p q r s t u v w x y z

Find the set of boxes that **first** fits into. Write **first** in the correct set of boxes.

Write the word to finish this sentence.

The _____ girl has the most hair.

SIGHT WORD

water

Trace the word **water**.

water water

Write the word **water** on the lines.

Drink **water** every day.

Circle the letters from the alphabet found in the word **water**.

a b c d e f g h i j k l m n o p q r s t u v w x y z

Find the set of boxes that **water** fits into. Write **water** in the correct set of boxes.

Write the word to finish this sentence.

Drink _____ every day.

SIGHT WORD

been

Trace the word **been**.

been been

Write the word **been** on the lines.

Have you **been** hugged today?

Circle the letters from the alphabet found in the word **been**.

a b c d e f g h i j k l m n o p q r s t u v w x y z

Find the set of boxes that **been** fits into. Write **been** in the correct set of boxes.

Write the word to finish this sentence.

Have you _____ hugged today?

SIGHT WORD

called

Trace the word **called**.

called

Write the word **called** on the lines.

This is **called** a circle.

Circle the letters from the alphabet found in the word **called**.

a b c d e f g h i j k l m n o p q r s t u v w x y z

Find the set of boxes that **called** fits into. Write **called** in the correct set of boxes.

Write the word to finish this sentence.

This is _____ a circle.

Name _____ Date _____

who

Trace the word **who**.

who who

Write the word **who** on the lines.

_____   _____

_____   _____

_____   _____

Who will buy these puppies?

Circle the letters from the alphabet found in the word **who**.

a b c d e f g h i j k l m n o p q r s t u v w x y z

Find the set of boxes that **who** fits into. Write **who** in the correct set of boxes.

Write the word to finish this sentence.

_____

_____ will buy these puppies?

SIGHT WORD

am

Trace the word **am**.

am am am

Write the word **am** on the lines.

_____   _____

_____   _____

_____   _____

I **am** getting
my doll fixed.

Circle the letters from the alphabet found in the word **am**.

a b c d e f g h i j k l m n o p q r s t u v w x y z

Find the set of boxes that **am** fits into. Write **am** in the correct set of boxes.

Write the word to finish this sentence.

I _____ getting my doll fixed.

SIGHT WORD

its

Trace the word **its**.

its its its

Write the word **its** on the lines.

_____ _____

_____ _____

_____ _____

Its tail is wagging.

Circle the letters from the alphabet found in the word **its**.

a b c d e f g h i j k l m n o p q r s t u v w x y z

Find the set of boxes that **its** fits into. Write **its** in the correct set of boxes.

Write the word to finish this sentence.

_____ tail is wagging.

SIGHT WORD

now

Trace the word **now**.

now now

Write the word **now** on the lines.

_____   _____

_____   _____

_____   _____

Now I'll read it.

Circle the letters from the alphabet found in the word **now**.

a b c d e f g h i j k l m n o p q r s t u v w x y z

Find the set of boxes that **now** fits into. Write **now** in the correct set of boxes.

Write the word to finish this sentence.

_____

_____ I'll read it.

SIGHT WORD

find

Trace the word **find**.

find find

Write the word **find** on the lines.

_____ _____

_____ _____

_____ _____

...6, 7, 8, 9, 10!

Will she **find** them?

Circle the letters from the alphabet found in the word **find**.

a b c d e f g h i j k l m n o p q r s t u v w x y z

Find the set of boxes that **find** fits into. Write **find** in the correct set of boxes.

Write the word to finish this sentence.

Will she _____ them?

SIGHT WORD

long

Trace the word **long**.

long long

Write the word **long** on the lines.

_____   _____

_____   _____

_____   _____

_____   _____

How **long** is the chain?

Circle the letters from the alphabet found in the word **long**.

a b c d e f g h i j k l m n o p q r s t u v w x y z

Find the set of boxes that **long** fits into. Write **long** in the correct set of boxes.

Write the word to finish this sentence.

How _____ is the chain?

SIGHT WORD

down

Trace the word **down**.

down down

Write the word **down** on the lines.

Put **down** that shoe!

Circle the letters from the alphabet found in the word **down**.

a b c d e f g h i j k l m n o p q r s t u v w x y z

Find the set of boxes that **down** fits into. Write **down** in the correct set of boxes.

Write the word to finish this sentence.

Put _____ that shoe!

SIGHT WORD

day

Trace the word **day**.

day day

Write the word **day** on the lines.

Do you like night or **day**?

Circle the letters from the alphabet found in the word **day**.

a b c d e f g h i j k l m n o p q r s t u v w x y z

Find the set of boxes that **day** fits into. Write **day** in the correct set of boxes.

Write the word to finish this sentence.

Do you like night or _____?

SIGH T
WORD

did

Trace the word **did**.

did   did

Write the word **did** on the lines.

_____   _____

_____   _____

_____   _____

Did you make
that hat?

Circle the letters from the alphabet found in the word **did**.

a b c d e f g h i j k l m n o p q r s t u v w x y z

Find the set of boxes that **did** fits into. Write **did** in the correct set of boxes.

Write the word to finish this sentence.

_____

_____ you make that hat?

SIGHT WORD

get

Trace the word **get**.

get   get

Write the word **get** on the lines.

Get some sleep.

Circle the letters from the alphabet found in the word **get**.

a b c d e f g h i j k l m n o p q r s t u v w x y z

Find the set of boxes that **get** fits into. Write **get** in the correct set of boxes.

Write the word to finish this sentence.

_____ some sleep.

SIGHT WORD

come

Trace the word **come**.

come come

Write the word **come** on the lines.

_____ _____

_____ _____

_____ _____

Come on in!

Circle the letters from the alphabet found in the word **come**.

a b c d e f g h i j k l m n o p q r s t u v w x y z

Find the set of boxes that **come** fits into. Write **come** in the correct set of boxes.

Write the word to finish this sentence.

_____

on in!

SIGHT WORD

made

Trace the word **made**.

made made

Write the word **made** on the lines.

Look at what she **made**.

Circle the letters from the alphabet found in the word **made**.

a b c d e f g h i j k l m n o p q r s t u v w x y z

Find the set of boxes that **made** fits into. Write **made** in the correct set of boxes.

Write the word to finish this sentence.

Look at what she _____.

SIGHT WORD

may

Trace the word **may**.

_____

may may

Write the word **may** on the lines.

_____   _____

_____   _____

_____   _____

You **may** eat
with me.

Circle the letters from the alphabet found in the word **may**.

a b c d e f g h i j k l m n o p q r s t u v w x y z

Find the set of boxes that **may** fits into. Write **may** in the correct set of boxes.

Write the word to finish this sentence.

You _____ eat with me.

SIGHT WORD

part

Trace the word **part**.

part part

Write the word **part** on the lines.

He will eat **part** of the sandwich.

Circle the letters from the alphabet found in the word **part**.

a b c d e f g h i j k l m n o p q r s t u v w x y z

Find the set of boxes that **part** fits into. Write **part** in the correct set of boxes.

Write the word to finish this sentence. _____

He will eat _____ of the sandwich.

Choose the Sight Word

Circle the word that completes each sentence.

I _____ to ride my bike.

did

like

. . . .

This is _____ a ladybug.

called

words

Choose the Sight Word

Circle the word that completes each sentence.

Do you like _____ new car?

they

his

What is _____ the box?

in

if

Choose the Sight Word

Circle the word that completes each sentence.

This _____ my toy.

is

number

. . . .

She likes to _____ at bugs.

make

look

Choose the Sight Word

Circle the word that completes each sentence.

We have fun ____ the beach.

at

and

. . . .

Cory will ____ swimming today.

these

go

Choose the Sight Word

Circle the word that completes each sentence.

The boy _____ sing.

could

been

_____ does she do that?

Its

How

Choose the Sight Word

Circle the word that completes each sentence.

Where will the ship go _____?

now

no

There are _____ balls.

from

two

Choose the Sight Word

Circle the word that completes each sentence.

It does _____ walk fast.

have

not

I feed my dog twice _____ day.

each

many

Choose the Sight Word

Circle the word that completes each sentence.

_____ is my school.

This

Than

_____ will the plane land?

When

Will

Choose the Sight Word

Circle the word that completes each sentence.

He gave _____ a card.

her

all

She is making it _____ herself.

had

by

Choose the Sight Word

Circle the word that completes each sentence.

_____ are two cats in the box.

Write

There

- -

_____ look silly!

I

My

Choose the Sight Word

Circle the word that completes each sentence.

He _____ his name.

come

said

Do you _____ the nest?

see

long

Choose the Sight Word

Circle the word that completes each sentence.

_____ took a nap.

Your

He

The animals _____ sounds.

people

made

Choose the Sight Word

Circle the word that completes each sentence.

_____ baby is sleeping.

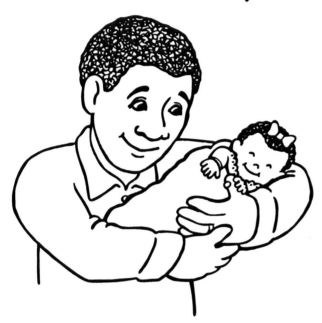

The

About

_____ is this boy doing?

Water

What

Choose the Sight Word

Circle the word that completes each sentence.

_____ jumped far!

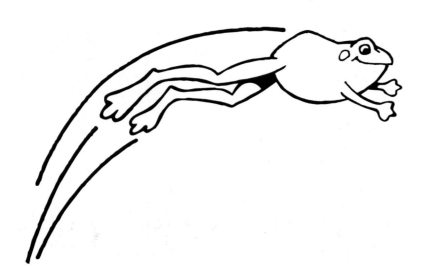

For

It

The bug is on _____ bush.

a

am

Choose the Sight Word

Circle the word that completes each sentence.

_____ will save the cat?

Who

Part

It's _____ to go!

time

other

Choose the Sight Word

Circle the word that completes each sentence.

Would you like _____?

with

some

We _____ climb the tree.

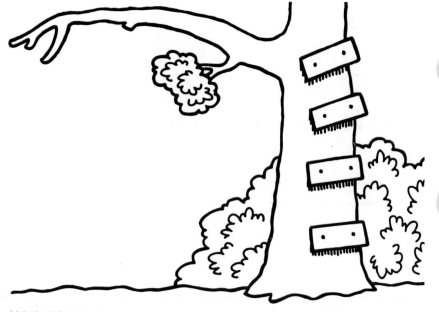

can

day

Flash Cards

the	in	he
of	is	was
and	you	for
a	that	on
to	it	are

Flash Cards (cont.)

as	at	or
with	be	one
his	this	had
they	have	by
I	from	words

Flash Cards (cont.)

but	we	there
not	when	use
what	your	an
all	can	each
were	said	which

Flash Cards *(cont.)*

she	will	many
do	up	then
how	other	them
their	about	these
if	out	so

Flash Cards *(cont.)*

some	him	two
her	into	more
would	time	write
make	has	go
like	look	see

Flash Cards _(cont.)_

number	my	called
no	than	who
way	first	am
could	water	its
people	been	now

Flash Cards *(cont.)*

find	get
long	come
down	made
day	may
did	part

Meeting Standards

Each activity meets the following Common Core State Standards © Copyright 2010. National Governors Association Center for Best Practices and Council of Chief State School Officers. All rights reserved. For more information about the Common Core State Standards, go to *http://www.corestandards.org/* or *http://www.teachercreated.com/standards/*.

Grade K

Reading: Foundational Skills	Pages
Print Concepts	
ELA.RF.K.1: Demonstrate understanding of the organization and basic features of print.	5–54
Phonics and Word Recognition	
ELA.RF.K.3: Know and apply grade-level phonics and word analysis skills in decoding words.	5–54, 105–120
Language	**Pages**
Conventions of Standard English	
ELA.L.K.1: Demonstrate command of the conventions of standard English grammar and usage when writing or speaking.	5–54

Grade 1

Reading: Foundational Skills	Pages
Print Concepts	
ELA.RF.1.1: Demonstrate understanding of the organization and basic features of print.	55–104
Phonics and Word Recognition	
ELA.RF.1.3: Know and apply grade-level phonics and word analysis skills in decoding words.	55–120
Language	**Pages**
Conventions of Standard English	
ELA.L.1.2: Demonstrate command of the conventions of standard English capitalization, punctuation, and spelling when writing.	55–104